D1716731

Childhoods
of the
Presidents

Abraham
Lincoln

Childhoods of the Presidents

John Adams

George W. Bush

Bill Clinton

Ulysses S. Grant

Andrew Jackson

Thomas Jefferson

John F. Kennedy

Abraham Lincoln

James Madison

James Monroe

Ronald Reagan

Franklin D. Roosevelt

Theodore Roosevelt

Harry S. Truman

George Washington

Woodrow Wilson

Abraham Lincoln

Bethanne Kelly Patrick

Mason Crest Publishers
Philadelphia

Produced by OTTN Publishing, Stockton, New Jersey

Mason Crest Publishers
370 Reed Road
Broomall, PA 19008
www.masoncrest.com

 Printed and bound in the Hashemite Kingdom of Jordan.

First printing

1 3 5 7 9 8 6 4 2

Library of Congress Cataloging-in-Publication Data

Patrick, Bethanne Kelly.
Abraham Lincoln / Bethanne Patrick.
p. cm. (Childhood of the presidents)
Summary: A biography of the sixteenth president of the United States, focusing on his childhood and young adulthood.
Includes bibliographical references (p.) and index.
ISBN 1-59084-275-8 (hc.)
1. Lincoln, Abraham, 1809-1865—Juvenile literature.
2. Lincoln, Abraham, 1809-1865—Childhood and youth—Juvenile literature. 3. Presidents—United States—Biography—Juvenile literature. [1. Lincoln, Abraham, 1809-1865—Childhood and youth. 2. Presidents.] I. Title. II. Series.
E457.905. P28 2003

2002023557

Publisher's note: All quotations in this book come from original sources, and contain the spelling and grammatical inconsistencies of the original text.

Childhoods
of the
𝒫residents

Table of Contents

★★★★★★★★★★★★★★★★★

★ *Introduction* ★

Alexis de Tocqueville began his great work *Democracy in America* with a discourse on childhood. If we are to understand the prejudices, the habits and the passions that will rule a man's life, Tocqueville said, we must watch the baby in his mother's arms; we must see the first images that the world casts upon the mirror of his mind; we must hear the first words that awaken his sleeping powers of thought. "The entire man," he wrote, "is, so to speak, to be seen in the cradle of the child."

That is why these books on the childhoods of the American presidents are so much to the point. And, as our history shows, a great variety of childhoods can lead to the White House. The record confirms the ancient adage that every American boy, no matter how unpromising his beginnings, can aspire to the presidency. Soon, one hopes, the adage will be extended to include every American girl.

All our presidents thus far have been white males who, within the limits of their gender, reflect the diversity of American life. They were born in nineteen of our states; eight of the last thirteen presidents were born west of the Mississippi. Of all our presidents, Abraham Lincoln had the least promising childhood, yet he became our greatest president. Oddly enough, presidents who are children of privilege sometimes feel an obligation to reform society in order to give children of poverty a better break. And, with Lincoln the great exception, presidents who are children of poverty sometimes feel that there is no need to reform a society that has enabled them to rise from privation to the summit.

Does schooling make a difference? Harry S. Truman, the only twentieth-century president never to attend college, is generally accounted a near-great president. Actually nine—more than one fifth—of our presidents never went to college at all, including such luminaries as George Washington, Andrew Jackson and Grover Cleveland. But, Truman aside, all the non-college men held the highest office before the twentieth century, and, given the increasing complexity of life, a college education will unquestionably be a necessity in the twenty-first century.

Every reader of this book, girls included, has a right to aspire to the presidency. As you survey the childhoods of those who made it, try to figure out the qualities that brought them to the White House. I would suggest that among those qualities are ambition, determination, discipline, education—and luck.

—ARTHUR M. SCHLESINGER, JR.

Near-Death Experience

*I*t was a warm Sunday afternoon in the early summer of 1814. Two young boys played together in the Kentucky wilderness. The younger of the boys, named Abraham, told his friend that a day earlier he had seen some *partridges* in the area. He suggested to his friend, whose name was Austin Gollaher, that they cross a nearby creek to hunt for the birds.

The two boys would have to walk across a narrow log to reach the other side of the creek. Normally, the stream was not very deep, but heavy rains a few days earlier had swollen the waters. As they crossed the log, six-year-old Abraham lost his balance. With a cry, he fell into the rushing water.

Neither of the two boys could swim. Austin rushed to the bank, found a long branch, and held it out to his friend. The frightened boy grasped the end of the branch, and Austin pulled him to shore. "He was almost dead and I was badly scared," Austin later remembered.

Visitors to the Lincoln Memorial in Washington, D.C., frequently come away with a sense of awe. Abraham Lincoln emerged from a humble, even impoverished background to become one of the greatest figures America has ever produced.

A sea of humanity surrounded the Lincoln Memorial for Martin Luther King's 1963 "I Have a Dream" speech. The location for this milestone in the civil rights movement was particularly fitting, given Lincoln's devotion to equality.

The soaked boy had swallowed a lot of river water, and Austin did not think Abraham was breathing when he was pulled ashore. "I rolled and pounded him in good earnest," Austin recalled. "Then I got him by the arms and shook him, the water meanwhile pouring out of his mouth. By this means I succeeded in bringing him to and he was soon all right."

Safe from drowning, the boys had another problem on their hands: the anger of their parents. "If our mothers discovered our wet clothes, they would whip us," Austin said. "This we dreaded from experience and determined to avoid." The two youngsters came up with a solution. "It was June, the sun was very warm, and we soon dried our clothing by spreading it on the rocks about us," Austin said. "We promised never to tell the story."

Life on the American *frontier* was hard, and childhood play could quickly turn dangerous. Yet Austin's playmate shrugged off the incident of his near drowning. He would go on to become a good woodsman, a respected attorney, and an honest politician. More than 45 years after being saved from drowning by Austin Gollaher, he would be elected the 16th president of the United States. Today, he is remembered as one of the nation's most beloved leaders—Abraham Lincoln.

A replica of the Lincolns' home near Knob Creek, Kentucky. The log cabins in which Abraham grew up were small (measuring about 16 by 18 feet) and stark, with a single window and door.

A Log Cabin in Kentucky

*T*he boy who would become the 16th president of the United States never knew his grandfather, although he had been named for him. The elder Abraham Lincoln (who also spelled his name Linkhorn and Linkern) had been a captain in the Virginia militia during the American Revolution. He was also a good friend of the woodsman Daniel Boone, who had pioneered a trail, known as the Wilderness Road, to the western frontier. At Boone's urging, Abraham had moved his wife and five children—including their four-year-old son Thomas—to Kentucky in 1782.

At the time, Kentucky was the wild edge of the American frontier. In fact, four years later, in May 1786, Native American warriors killed Abraham in a surprise attack. His sons, including eight-year-old Thomas, witnessed the slaying. Years later Thomas told this story to his own son Abraham, who would eventually write, "My *paternal* grandfather, Abraham Lincoln, emigrated from Rockingham County, Virginia, to Kentucky, about 1781 or 2, where, a year or two later, he was killed by Indians, not in battle, but by stealth, when he was laboring to open a farm in the forest."

Abraham Lincoln's ancestry can be traced to Samuel Lincoln, a weaver's apprentice who emigrated from Hingham, England, to Hingham, Massachusetts, in the early 18th century.

When he grew older, Thomas Lincoln worked for his uncle Isaac as a hired hand in Tennessee. He moved back to Kentucky in 1802. The next year he purchased a large farm near Elizabethtown. Thomas found work as a carpenter and cabinetmaker. Around this time he met a woman named Nancy Hanks.

Like Thomas Lincoln, Nancy had been a child when her family traveled over the Wilderness Road through the Cumberland Gap into Kentucky. Nancy was kind and deeply religious. As an adult she became a skilled *seamstress*. She and Thomas Lincoln were married on June 12, 1806.

After the wedding the couple lived in a log cabin in Elizabethtown. In 1807, Nancy Lincoln gave birth to a daughter, Sarah. Soon after this they moved to another small log cabin, located on Nolin Creek near Hodgenville, in Hardin County, Kentucky. There, on February 12, 1809, Nancy gave birth to their second child, a son they named Abraham.

The next day Nancy's cousin Dennis Hanks had a chance to hold the infant. In an 1865 letter he remembered the moment. "He looked jist like any other baby at fust, like a red cherry-pulp squeezed dry in wrinkles. An he didn't improve none as he growed older. Abe was never much for looks."

Thomas and Nancy Lincoln had to work hard and long to support their family. Abraham's father took whatever carpentry work he could find to earn money. Abraham's mother ran the household and raised the children. She did the best she

"All that I am or hope ever to be I get from my mother," Abraham Lincoln would say of Nancy Hanks Lincoln (left), a gentle, deeply religious woman. His father, Thomas Lincoln (right), eked out a meager living as a farmer and carpenter.

could with the little she had, making clothes as quickly as Abraham outgrew them.

The *settlers* living on the frontier during the early years of the 19th century faced many hardships and dangers. Finding sources of water wasn't always easy, and once those were found settlers had to *forage* for food. People worked long hours cutting down trees and clearing land to build shelter. They used the trees they felled as construction material. Small log cabins could be put together quickly. "We was all pore, them days," recalled Dennis Hanks. "But the Lincolns was poorer than anybody. Choppin' trees, an' grubbin' roots, an' splittin' rails, an' huntin', an' trappin' didn't leave Tom no time to put a . . . floor in his cabin. It was all he could do to git his family enough to eat and kiver 'em."

In spite of hardships, settlers like the Lincolns continued to move to the frontier territories. They also moved around once they had arrived, looking for the best land to claim. In 1811, when Abraham was just a toddler, his father decided to transplant his family to Knob Creek, Kentucky, just a few miles away. There he staked out a large farm. Abraham later said his earliest memories were of the home at Knob Creek.

As he grew older, Abraham enjoyed spending time in the woods. He fished in the creek, set traps for rabbits and muskrats, and went raccoon hunting with his father and cousin Dennis. Around the farm, he had many chores: carrying buckets of water, keeping the wood-box filled with fuel for the stove, cleaning the fireplace, and gathering nuts and berries. Abraham also helped his father plant crops.

Thomas and Nancy Lincoln took their family to church regularly. At home, Nancy Lincoln read Bible stories to her children. Abraham was fascinated by the stories. After he and his sister learned to read, they took turns reading the stories on Sundays when there was no church service.

Literacy was not widespread on the frontier. Thomas Lincoln couldn't read but could sign his name with effort. Nancy Hanks Lincoln could read a little but, like many other settlers, could only make a rough mark as a signature.

The Lincolns also were *abolitionists*. They believed slavery was evil and that all people should be free. As Abraham was growing up, the United States was divided over the idea of slavery. The first black slaves had been brought from Africa to North America during the early 17th century. By the time of Abraham's birth it was illegal to bring new slaves to the United States. However, millions of African-American men and women, descended from these earlier slaves, continued to live in *bondage* in the southern states.

As the United States pushed its boundaries west, a debate arose over slavery. Wealthy slaveholders living in the southern states wanted slavery to be permitted in new states added to the Union. This would help ensure that the system of slavery on which they had built their fortunes would be preserved. People who believed slavery was wrong hoped it would one day be illegal throughout the United States. In the meantime, they didn't want to see slavery spread into new states.

Abraham Lincoln later said that he was "naturally anti-slavery" and could not remember a time when he "did not so think, and feel."

Abraham had his first chance for education while the family lived at Knob Creek. When there was no pressing work to be done, Abraham walked two miles to the schoolhouse, where he learned the basics of reading, writing, and arithmetic. Young Abraham and his sister Sarah were sent for short periods to "blab schools" run by Zachariah Riney, and later by Caleb Hazel. They were called "blab schools" because of the noise. Students were required to recite their lessons out loud while the schoolmaster instructed other students.

Abraham would not spend much time in school, however. His parents believed Kentucky was becoming more and more populated with people who supported slavery. The Lincolns felt it was time to move.

Hard Times

ive years after moving to Knob Creek, Thomas Lincoln sold his lands and moved his family into the untracked wilderness of Indiana across the Ohio River. The Northwest Land Ordinance of 1787 made slavery illegal in Indiana. It was 1816, and Abraham was eight. He later recalled that the family moved "partly on account of slavery, but chiefly on account of difficulty of land titles in Kentucky." It was easier to prove land ownership in Indiana than it was in Kentucky.

The perilous journey took seven days, and the Lincolns lost some of their belongings in a *flatboat* accident on the river. The nearest neighbor in Indiana lived two miles distant, and it was necessary to put up some kind of lodging as quickly as possible. When the Lincolns arrived in Spencer County, it was late fall, and there was time only to pull together a "half-faced camp"—a crude three-sided shelter of logs, brush, and leaves.

Abraham Lincoln and his family were well acquainted with hardship, particularly after his mother's death in 1818. Seen here among some household items that have survived are two of the very few luxuries the Lincoln family possessed: a small mirror and a chessboard.

A blazing fire warmed the open side. Thomas Lincoln constructed the camp of unfinished poles, intending to spend the winter making finished slabs for a cabin.

The only water was nearly a mile away. For food the family depended almost entirely on game. Their backyard was "unbroken forest," Lincoln wrote, and one of his jobs was to help clear trees. In his autobiography, he wrote, "Abraham, though very young, was large of his age, and had an ax put into his hands at once, and from that till within his twenty-third year he was almost constantly handling that most useful instrument—less, of course, in plowing and harvesting seasons."

Thomas and Abraham began building a better home and preparing the land for planting. They built a cabin, which measured 16 by 18 feet, near Little Pigeon Creek. This crude dwelling had one door and one window. Glass was not available in the wilderness of Indiana, so for windowpanes Thomas Lincoln used the skin of a pig, which had been dried and stretched thin so it was *translucent*. The family possessed a few pots and pans. Thomas and Abraham together made a crude table and four chairs, as well as a bedstead. That was all the furniture they had.

Abraham Lincoln remembered Indiana as a "wild region, with many bears and other wild animals still in the woods." In

Abraham and Sarah Lincoln had a younger brother, Thomas, who was born in 1817 but died in infancy.

his autobiography, he told of shooting a wild turkey, but wrote that he "has never since pulled a trigger on any larger game." When the men

A page from Thomas Lincoln's family Bible. After the death of his illiterate father in 1851, Abraham wrote down important dates in the family's history. In the second entry he recorded his own birth.

could not catch any game, the Lincolns lived on "hoecake" made from cornmeal and water.

During the long winter nights in the new cabin, Abraham read often from the family's three books: a Bible, a *catechism*, and a spelling book. He soon memorized sections of these books. He read by the light of the fire. Abraham also practiced the *penmanship* he had learned in school. He wrote with a charred stick on a piece of tree bark, or on slabs of wood.

In the summer of 1818, a deadly disease known as "milk sickness" struck the region. The disease was called milk sickness because people caught it after drinking the milk of cows that had eaten a poisonous plant. The first case struck almost 20 miles away, but it was near enough to cause alarm for the Lincolns. First Nancy's uncle and aunt, who lived nearby, were stricken and died. Then Nancy herself contracted milk sickness. Ill for a week, she died on October 5, 1818, at the age of 34. Before she died, Nancy called her son and daughter to her bedside and urged them to be good to their father, each other, and their fellows.

Because she died at a young age, Nancy Hanks Lincoln represents to some the sadness of all mothers who do not live to see their children as grown people. Poet Rosemary Benet wrote "Nancy Hanks," and poet Julius Silberger wrote "A Reply to Nancy Hanks." You can find these poems in your library or online.

Nancy Hanks and her aunt and uncle were buried on a knoll not far from their homes, without any religious service. Several months later, a traveling preacher named Parson Elkins delivered a funeral sermon for them.

Abraham Lincoln was just nine years old at the time of

his mother's death. His mother's cousin Dennis Hanks, who was living with the family at the time, later recalled that after Nancy's death, Abraham became more of a thinker. Perhaps it was the sadness of losing her that made him more interested in ideas, and less interested in farming. Years later, when he was working as a lawyer in

On the American frontier, family Bibles represented more than reading material. Bibles often carried records of births, marriages, deaths, landholdings, and more. They were passed from generation to generation, and are sometimes the only record historians have of events, relationships, and transactions.

Illinois, he told his friend and law partner William Herndon, "All that I am or hope ever to be I get from my mother. God bless her."

After Nancy Lincoln's death, the burden of running the household fell on the shoulders of 12-year-old Sarah. She could scarcely handle cooking and cleaning for her father and cousin Dennis as well as her younger brother. When Sarah was exhausted, Abraham would try to cheer her up. Once he brought her a baby raccoon. He also helped with domestic chores like starting the cooking fire.

Thomas Lincoln and Dennis Hanks had to labor at farming and hunting in order to provide the family with food. Although Abraham and his sister tried, and everyone continued to work hard, the Lincoln home was soon reduced to near-squalor. Sarah and Abraham had no new clothes. The clothes they owned were too small and had been worn nearly to rags.

Realizing that his children needed a mother and he needed a wife, Thomas eventually returned to Kentucky and married a woman named Sarah Bush Johnston. Thomas had known Sarah Bush when they were younger, but she had since married a man named Daniel Johnston. He had died in 1816, leaving her a widow with three children. She was working as a servant in the home of Samuel Haycraft when Thomas Lincoln arrived. Haycraft wrote:

> [Thomas Lincoln] made a very short courtship. He came to see her on the first day of December 1819, and in a straight forward manner told her . . . 'Miss Johnston . . . I have no wife and you no husband. I came a-purpose to marry you. I knowed you from a gal and you knowed me from a boy. I've no time to lose, and if you're willin', let it be done straight off.' She replied that she could not marry him right off as she had some little debts which she wanted to pay first. He replied, 'Give me a list of them.' He got the list and paid them that evening. Next morning, I issued the license and they were married within sixty yards of my house.

Sarah Bush Lincoln owned enough furniture that her new husband needed to hire a four-horse team to haul it back to Little Pigeon Creek. She had a bureau that cost $40, a clothes chest, a table and six chairs, as well as bedding, crockery, tinware, and ironware.

After Sarah and her children arrived at the Lincoln farm, she set about cleaning, repairing, and cooking. In a very short time the family had a true home. She made a real floor for the cabin, and had Thomas travel to buy real doors and window sashes. Dennis Hanks wrote, "In a few weeks all had changed, and where everything was wanting now all was snug and comfortable." Sarah, whom he called "a woman of great ener-

Sarah Bush Johnston Lincoln called her stepson Abraham "the best boy I have ever seen." For his part, Abe Lincoln would in later years remember Sarah as "my angel mother."

gy," also worked to make all six of the children in the house (her children John, Sarah, and Matilda; Abraham and Sarah Lincoln; and Dennis Hanks) one family. Dennis said, "The two sets of children got along finely together, as if they had been children of the same parents." Abraham learned to love his new stepparent and in later years referred to her as "my angel mother."

Sarah Lincoln was equally fond of Abraham, whom she called "the best boy I have ever seen." She was able to read and write, and she understood how much he loved to read and to study. When a small school opened near his family's home, Sarah Lincoln urged him to attend. She told him, "A poor chance to learn is better than none."

This painting, titled *Boyhood of Lincoln*, depicts the youth reading by firelight. "I sometimes wish he liked work as much as he does a book," Thomas Lincoln once complained about his studious son.

Living and Learning

*I*n the early decades of the 19th century, it was difficult for youngsters living on the frontier to get an education. Abraham Lincoln would later write, "There were some schools, so called; but no qualification was ever required of a teacher beyond readin', writin', and cipherin' to the Rule of Three. If a straggler supposed to understand Latin happened to sojourn in the neighborhood, he was looked upon as a wizzard [*sic*]. There was absolutely nothing to excite ambition for education.

"Of course when I came of age I did not know much," he continued. "Still somehow, I could read, write, and cipher to the Rule of Three; but that was all. I have not been to school since. The little advance I now have upon this store of education, I have picked up from time to time under the pressure of necessity."

If there was little education to be had, there were even fewer school supplies. When the sun went down, Abraham had to read by dim firelight. He had no paper notebooks or ink pens, so he practiced math equations by scratching with a piece of coal on the back of a shovel. When he did get his hands on some paper, he bound several pieces together with a piece of string to make his own "sum book."

The school at Pigeon Creek lasted only a few weeks, as did the two later schools Abraham attended. In all, this future president had less than a year's worth of formal education. Yet nothing made young Abraham happier than a book. "He cares for a book more than anything else," complained his father. "I sometimes wish he liked work as much as he does a book." Abraham borrowed books from neighbors, including *Aesop's Fables*, *Robinson Crusoe*, and *Pilgrim's Progress*. To him, books were treasures that were hard to come by and needed to be read and reread.

When he was 16, Abraham Lincoln borrowed a book called *Life of Washington*, by Parson Mason Weems, from a neighbor named Josiah Crawford. During a rainstorm, the book accidentally became soaked. Abraham told his neighbor exactly what had happened and promised to work for Crawford until he had paid for the book. *Life of Washington* became the first book Abraham Lincoln ever owned.

Many folk beliefs persisted in the early West, where life was hard and education in short supply. Sometimes this "wisdom" was contradictory. For example, one belief was that it was bad luck for a bird to fly into the house, while another belief held that a bird coming into the house would bring good luck.

This may have been one of the incidents that led to the nickname "Honest Abe." Another had occurred when he was about nine and attending a school near his home on the Little Pigeon Creek. The schoolteacher had hung a large set of deer antlers over the entrance to the classroom. When the teacher left the room for a few moments, Abraham decided to show off. He walked to the doorway, jumped up, grabbed the antlers, and swung back and forth. Suddenly the horns broke, and Abraham tumbled to the ground. He hurried back to his seat as the teacher returned to the room. The angry teacher demanded to know who had done the damage.

> Abraham Lincoln was an excellent writer; his speeches are still studied. His most famous is the Gettysburg Address, a short speech he delivered at the dedication of a cemetery for fallen soldiers at Gettysburg, Pennsylvania, in November 1863.

Abraham admitted his guilt immediately. "I did it, sir," he answered, "but I didn't mean to. I just hung on it and it broke." He was punished for his behavior, but stories like this would eventually lead to his reputation for honesty.

Just as young Abraham enjoyed reading stories, he enjoyed telling stories also. "When he appeared in company, the boys would gather and cluster around him to hear him talk," one of his school friends later remembered. "He made fun and cracked his jokes making all happy. But the jokes and fun were at no man's expense. He wounded no man's feelings. . . . He naturally assumed the leadership of the boys."

Lincoln told some stories about himself. For example, he described how, when he was 10 years old, he had been kicked by a neighbor's horse and knocked unconscious. He used to claim that he had been "killed for a time" and brought back to life.

Tall, strong, and handy with an ax, the teenaged Abraham Lincoln earned 25 cents a day splitting logs for 10-foot-long fence rails. He could make up to 400 of the rails in a single day.

As a teenager, Abraham grew quickly. By the time he was 17 years old, he stood 6 feet 4 inches tall. He was much taller and stronger than the other boys. He could wield his ax with great power, and he often found work splitting long logs into wooden rails for fences. The fence rails that Abraham Lincoln split were about 10 feet long and four inches wide. He could make about 400 rails in a day—a job for which he was paid 25 cents.

His stepmother sometimes teased Abraham about his height. She told him that it didn't matter if his feet were dirty, because she could always scrub the floor, but warned him that he had to wash his head or the *whitewashed* ceiling of the cabin would become dirty. This gave Abraham an idea for a joke. He asked some young children playing near the house to walk through a mud puddle. Then he took each one, turned them upside down, and walked them across the ceiling.

"Aunt Sairy come in, an' it was so blamed funny she set down an' laughed, though she said Abe'd oughter be spanked," remembered Abraham's cousin Dennis Hanks. "I don't know how far he had to go fur more lime, but he white-washed the ceilin' all over again."

Abraham took a job with James Taylor, who owned a farm on the Anderson Creek near where it joined the Ohio River. The Ohio was an important waterway that joined the Mississippi, linking the northern states with the port of New Orleans. Abraham also worked as a ferryman on the river, and by the time he was 18 years old he had built his own boat and gone into business for himself. He took passengers to steamships waiting in the river, and brought them from the

In 1828 an Indiana merchant hired Abraham Lincoln to take a flatboat of supplies down the Mississippi River to New Orleans. Abraham had previously worked as a ferryman on the Ohio River. This illustration is from a 19th-century book about Lincoln's life.

boats to shore. Once, after moving two travelers and their trunks out to a waiting boat, he was paid with two bright silver half-dollar coins. "You may think it was a very little thing," he later said, "but it was a most important incident in my life. I could scarcely credit that I—the poor boy—had earned a dollar in less than a day; that by honest work I had earned a dollar."

Unfortunately, later that day Abraham accidentally dropped one of the coins over the side of his boat. "I can see the quivering and shining of that half-dollar yet," he said. "In the quick current it went down the stream and sunk from my sight forever."

As Abraham was growing up, the region of Indiana where the family lived had also grown. The general store owned by James Gentry became a trading center around which the village of Gentryville grew. In the fall of 1828, Gentry decided to send a flatboat of supplies to New Orleans. He hoped to trade the pork, flour, bacon, produce, and livestock for manufactured items, such as pots and pans, soap, and cloth. These would be brought back to Gentryville, where he could sell them in his store.

Gentry hired Abraham Lincoln to help build the boat and to guide it to New Orleans. James Gentry's son Allen would also go along. This trip would be the first time the 19-year-old country boy ever saw a city. While Lincoln's autobiographical writings give few details about the trip, the fact that he mentions it shows how significant it must have been for him. He does write about how the boat was attacked by seven men "with intent to kill and rob." Abraham was cut during the fight, but he and Allen Gentry managed to drive off their attackers, then pole their boat away from the shore. Abraham's cut healed, leaving a permanent scar on his face.

When Abraham and Allen arrived in New Orleans, they sold or traded their cargo and even their boat. With their new supplies for James Gentry's store, they booked passage on a steamboat traveling back up the Mississippi. As they were headed home in February of 1829, Abraham celebrated his 20th birthday. When he got home, he was paid $24 for the three-month trip. He gave the money to his father and went back to work on the farm.

But Abraham Lincoln had seen that there was more to life than the backwoods communities he had grown up in. He looked forward to his 21st birthday—the day when he would be considered an adult and could leave home to find his own way in the world.

Abraham Lincoln, 16th president of the United States, led the nation through its most serious crisis.

A New Life in Illinois

arly in 1830, Thomas Lincoln sold his Indiana farm and again moved his family, to a new home in Illinois. He built a cabin on the Sangamon River, not far from his relative by marriage, John Hanks. After the first summer there, the Lincolns moved again, this time to Coles County, Illinois. But Abraham did not go along. He was now 21 years old—the official age of adulthood—and thus independent. He and two friends had agreed to take a cargo of produce, belonging to a man named Denton Offutt, to New Orleans.

After the trip to New Orleans was successfully completed, Offutt placed Abraham in charge of the mill and store he owned in New Salem, Illinois. At the time New Salem was little more than a street overlooking the Sangamon River. But for Abraham, it represented the start of a new life.

In 1832, a group of Sac and Fox Indians who had been forced from their tribal lands in Illinois returned to the state. Settlers in Illinois formed militias to fight the Native Americans and their chief, Black Hawk. The volunteers of the New Salem region elected Abraham Lincoln to be their captain. For three months they marched in search of the Sac and

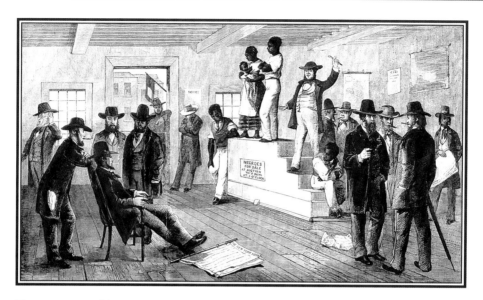

During one of his trips to New Orleans, Abraham Lincoln witnessed a slave auction. Seeing human beings bought and sold must have strengthened his early convictions against slavery. Eventually, slavery, America's "peculiar institution," provided the spark that ignited the Civil War.

Fox warriors, but Abraham never saw any fighting during the Black Hawk War.

When he returned home, he formed a partnership with a man named William Berry. Together, they purchased a store in New Salem. However, the two men were not successful in business. Abraham's next job was as postmaster of New Salem.

During this time Abraham had become interested in politics. He had run for a seat in the state *legislature* in 1832, but lost. In 1834 he won a seat in the legislature. His campaign impressed John Stuart, a political leader and lawyer in Springfield, Illinois. Stuart convinced Abraham to read all the law books he could buy or borrow and become a lawyer. In September 1836 Abraham passed the bar examinations and was admitted to practice. He moved to Springfield, the new state capital, to become Stuart's law partner.

In 1839, while living in Springfield, Abraham met a pretty woman named Mary Todd. They were married on November 4, 1842. Their first child, Robert, was born in 1843, and they bought a home in Springfield the following year. That same year Abraham formed a law practice with William Herndon, who became a good friend.

Abraham also continued his political career, being reelected to the state legislature in 1836, 1838, and 1840. In 1846 he was elected to the U.S. Congress.

Abraham Lincoln had always viewed slavery as a "moral, social and political wrong" and looked forward to its eventual abolition. As a congressman, he tried to introduce a bill to abolish slavery in the District of Columbia. This was unsuccessful, and he was not elected to a second term in Congress.

The Lincoln family continued to grow. In 1846 a second son, Edward, was born. He died of an illness in 1850, at age four. That same year a third child, William, was born, and in 1853 the Lincolns welcomed their fourth child, Thomas (nicknamed Tad).

In 1858, Abraham ran for the U.S. Senate against Stephen A. Douglas. The two men held a series of debates across Illinois, discussing the issue of slavery. Although Abraham lost the election, the debates brought him national attention. When the Republican National Convention met to choose its presidential candidate in 1860, Abraham Lincoln was nominated. In the election, he received the largest number of votes and became the 16th president of the United States.

The states of the South were afraid Lincoln would try to

make slavery illegal. A number of states decided to *secede* from the United States. They announced that they would form a new country, the Confederate States of America. In April 1861, Confederate troops fired on a Federal garrison at Fort Sumter, South Carolina. The Civil War had begun.

From that point on, President Lincoln was committed to war in order to end the southern rebellion. Although at first the Confederate troops seemed to have the advantage, the tide soon turned for the Union. After the battle of Antietam in September 1862, Abraham decided to issue his *Emancipation* Proclamation. This was a statement that said all slaves in the rebellious states would be freed.

In the summer of 1863, the Union army won several major battles, at Gettysburg, Pennsylvania, and at Vicksburg,

Scenes of the Civil War: (above) Lincoln with General George B. McClellan and other Union army leaders, 1862; (opposite top) a painting of the fierce fighting at Gettysburg; (opposite bottom) dead Confederate soldiers lie on a battlefield. A half million men lost their lives as a result of the Civil War, making it the bloodiest conflict in U.S. history. Yet, thanks in large measure to the wisdom and leadership of Abraham Lincoln, the Union survived.

Mississippi. In November 1863 President Lincoln traveled to Gettysburg to dedicate a cemetery for the soldiers who had been killed there. He gave a famous speech, explaining that the Civil War was a struggle to preserve a nation "conceived in liberty, and dedicated to the proposition that all men are created equal." His Gettysburg Address remains one of the most famous American speeches.

Despite the demands of the presidency, Abraham continued to be an active, loving father. He enjoyed playing with his sons on the floor of their living quarters in the White House. Tad and Willie liked to play pranks, and their father usually laughed and refused to discipline them. Their antics must have provided the president welcome relief from the pressures of waging the Civil War.

In 1864, Abraham Lincoln was elected to a second term as president. His second inaugural address was brief. The speech urged all Americans "to bind up the nation's wounds." Americans could achieve a just and lasting peace by acting "with malice toward none; with charity for all," he said.

By the spring of 1865, the Civil War was practically over. On April 9, Confederate general Robert E. Lee surrendered his army at Appomattox Court House, Virginia. Although fighting continued in some areas for a few months, the Confederacy was no more. The Union had been preserved.

Tragically, Abraham Lincoln would not live long enough to enjoy the result of his efforts. On the evening of April 14, 1865, he and his wife attended a play at Ford's Theatre in Washington, D.C. A man named John Wilkes Booth shot the president in the back of the head from close range. The presi-

dent never regained con-
sciousness, and died at 7:22
A.M. on April 15, 1865. He was
just 56 years old.

The Lincoln family would
suffer more than its share
of tragedy: Abraham was
assassinated shortly after
the Confederate surren-
der, Mrs. Lincoln became
insane, and only one of
their sons lived to adulthood.

A nation that had scarcely
begun to heal the wounds of
a long and terrible war was
stunned by this *assassina-
tion*. The public mourning for President Lincoln included a
large, formal funeral service. A train then carried his coffin
slowly back to his home in Illinois.

For nearly 150 years people have remained fascinated by
Abraham Lincoln. His leadership during the greatest crisis in
American history, and his efforts to abolish slavery, were great
accomplishments. The life of Abraham Lincoln is an example
of what determination, faith, and hard work can accomplish in
the United States.

CHRONOLOGY

1809 Abraham Lincoln is born February 12 in a one-room cabin on Nolin Creek in Kentucky.

1811 The Lincoln family moves to a large farm at Knob Creek.

1816 The Lincoln family crosses the Ohio River and settles in the backwoods of Indiana.

1818 Nancy Hanks Lincoln dies of milk sickness.

1819 Thomas Lincoln marries Sarah Bush Johnston.

1828 Abraham Lincoln and Allen Gentry take a cargo of produce on a flatboat to New Orleans.

1830 The Lincoln family moves to Illinois and settles on the Sangamon River near Decatur.

1831 The Lincoln family moves on, but Abraham stays in Illinois, settling in New Salem.

1832 Abraham Lincoln serves as a militia captain in the Black Hawk War.

1834 Elected to the Illinois state legislature.

1842 Marries Mary Todd on November 4.

1846 Abraham Lincoln elected to the U.S. House of Representatives.

1858 Gains national attention during campaign for U.S. Senate against Stephen A. Douglas.

1860 On November 6 Abraham Lincoln is elected president of the United States, winning 180 out of 303 electoral votes, and 40 percent of the popular vote.

1861 The Civil War begins.

1863 Lincoln issues the Emancipation Proclamation on January 1, freeing slaves in the rebellious states; the battle of Gettysburg marks a turning point in the Civil War.

1864 On November 8 Lincoln is elected to his second term as president, winning 212 out of 223 possible electoral votes and 55 percent of the popular vote.

1865 Confederate general Robert E. Lee surrenders his army to Union general Ulysses S. Grant at Appomattox Court House, Virginia, on April 9; on the evening of April 14 Abraham Lincoln is shot by John Wilkes Booth and dies the next morning.

abolitionist—someone who campaigned against slavery during the 18th and 19th centuries.

assassination—a murder by sudden or secret attack, usually in the service of a cause.

bondage—slavery or servitude.

catechism—a book containing questions and answers used to test the religious knowledge of a person of the Christian faith.

emancipation—the act of freeing from bondage or other controlling influence.

flatboat—a boat for use in shallow waters, with a flat bottom and squared-off ends; used for bulky freight.

forage—to search for food or supplies.

frontier—a region that forms the border of known, settled territory.

legislature—an official body, usually chosen by election, with the power to make laws.

partridge—a medium-sized ground nesting bird with variegated plumage, such as the ruffed grouse or bobwhite.

paternal—from the father's side of a family.

penmanship—the art, skill, or technique of writing by hand.

seamstress—a woman who sews for a living.

secede—to make a formal withdrawal of membership from an organization, state, or alliance.

settler—somebody who comes to live in a new place, especially a place that is unpopulated or populated by people of a different race or civilization.

translucent—allowing light to pass through, but only diffusely, so that objects on the other side cannot be clearly distinguished.

whitewash—a substance made of lime mixed with water and used like paint for whitening walls.

FURTHER READING

Burchard, Peter. *Lincoln & Slavery*. New York: Atheneum Press, 1999.

Freedman, Russell. *Lincoln: A Photobiography*. Boston: Houghton Mifflin, 1987.

Holzer, Harold. *Abraham Lincoln the Writer: A Treasury of His Great Speeches and Letters*. Honesdale, Pa.: Boyds Mill Press, 2000.

Jones, Lynda. *Abe Lincoln*. New York: Scholastic Trade, 2000.

Kigel, Richard. *The Frontier Years of Abraham Lincoln*. New York: Walker and Company, 1986.

Sandburg, Carl. *Abe Lincoln Grows Up*. New York: Harcourt Brace, 1987.

INTERNET RESOURCES

- http://www.nps.gov/abli/
  Abe Lincoln Birthplace National Historic Park

- http://www.historyplace.com
  Biography of Lincoln

- http://www.ipl.org/ref/POTUS/alincoln.html
  Fast Facts on Lincoln

- http://members.aol.com/RVSNorton/Lincoln.html
  Lincoln Links

- http://www.pbs.org/wgbh/amex/lincolns
  The Time of the Lincolns

INDEX

INDEX

PICTURE CREDITS

Contributors

ARTHUR M. SCHLESINGER JR. holds the Albert Schweitzer Chair in the Humanities at the Graduate Center of the City University of New York. He is the author of more than a dozen books, including *The Age of Jackson*; *The Vital Center*; *The Age of Roosevelt* (3 vols.); *A Thousand Days: John F. Kennedy in the White House*; *Robert Kennedy and His Times*; *The Cycles of American History*; and *The Imperial Presidency*. Professor Schlesinger served as  Special Assistant to President Kennedy (1961–63). His numerous awards include the Pulitzer Prize for History; the Pulitzer Prize for Biography; two National Book Awards; the Bancroft Prize; and the American Academy of Arts and Letters Gold Medal for History.

BETHANNE KELLY PATRICK is the author of several books for young readers, including *Ulysses S. Grant* in the series CHILDHOODS OF THE PRESIDENTS. She holds a master's degree in English from the University of Virginia and specializes in middle-school curricula. She is a freelance writer who lives with her husband and two daughters in Virginia.